DOUBLE, DOUBLE

A Play in One Act

by

JAMES SAUNDERS

SAMUEL   FRENCH

LONDON

W YORK   TORONTO   SYDNEY   HOLLYWOOD

MADE AND PRINTED IN GREAT BRITAIN BY
LATIMER TREND AND CO. LTD, WHITSTABLE
MADE IN ENGLAND

CHARACTERS

(in the order of their appearance)

GRUNGE, a bus driver

NELLIE, the cook

NIMROD, a bus driver

FRAN, the cleaner and kitchen hand

A BUS INSPECTOR

PUMFRET, Grunge's conductor

GIMLET, a bus driver

LILLIAN, Gimlet's conductress

IRIS, Dogg's conductress

BERT DOGG, a bus driver

The action of the Play passes in a busmen's canteen, about noon on a winter's day

Time—the present

NOTES

The pairs of characters bracketed together are doubled. Appearance, characterization and possibly accent should be such that each member of a pair is immediately recognizable while the common identity of the pair remains obvious.

The Inspector and Bert Dogg are burly men, compared with Gimlet and Nimrod. What is in Iris a young slimness has become in Fran an asexual wispiness. Nellie and Lillian are plump.

{ GRUNGE	Driver
{ PUMFRET	His conductor
{ NELLIE	The cook
{ LILLIAN	Gimlet's conductress
{ FRAN	Cleaner and kitchen hand
{ IRIS	Bert Dogg's conductress
{ INSPECTOR	Driver
{ BERT DOGG	
{ NIMROD	Driver
{ GIMLET	Driver

DOUBLE, DOUBLE

SCENE—*A busmen's canteen. About noon on a winter's day.*

The main door is R *and there is a window up* RC *in the back wall. A door* L *leads to other parts of the building and a third door, behind the counter, leads to the kitchen. The counter runs parallel to the back wall from the wall* L *to* C, *and has a flap at the right end giving access to the tables. The counter is set café-wise with biscuits, cheese rolls, etc. Behind the counter are shelves with cigarettes, matches, etc. There is a longish table* RC *with two chairs above it, two chairs below it and a chair at each end. A smaller table, with four chairs, is in the corner up* R. *There is a hat-stand down* R, *a pin-table below the door* L, *and a clock on the wall behind the counter. Other suitable dressing may be added at the discretion of the Producer.*

When the CURTAIN *rises,* GRUNGE, *a bus-driver, is seated alone above the right end of the table* RC, *finishing his dinner, which he eats moodily, casting a dark glance now and then at the clock and then at the plate of dinner set at the place* L *of him. After a few moments,* NELLIE *enters behind the counter.*

NELLIE. What do you want for sweet?

GRUNGE. Is that clock right, Nellie?

NELLIE. It's always right. There's fruit roll or jam tart.

GRUNG. Oh, I dunno. What's best?

NELLIE. One's hot, the other's cold.

GRUNGE. Hm! (*He indicates the plate of food at the place beside him*) Here, look at this. *Look* at it.

NELLIE. If your mate don't get here soon, his dinner'll be cold.

GRUNGE. What I'm *saying*. It's congealed. Look at the time. Two jiffs, he said he'd be. "Get my dinner for me," he says, "I'll be in in two jiffs." Quarter of an hour ago, that was. I dunno what he *does* out there. (*He checks the clock against his watch*)

NELLIE. Do you want it back on the hot-plate?

GRUNGE. Sitting there filling in his pools, I dare say.

NELLIE. Some people got no respect for a good meal. Might as well serve 'em bran-mash, some of 'em, they wouldn't know the difference. Look at it, going to waste. I tell you this: if he comes in complaining his dinner's cold, it'll be the finish. I've had enough complaining in this establishment. I've been back to the cardboard factory once and I can go back again, any day of the week.

GRUNGE. It's his stomach I'm thinking of.

NELLIE. Decent kitchens they got there, *and* the pay's good, *and* the hours are regular. It'll be the finish, you can tell your mate that from me.

GRUNGE. We're due out in a few minutes. He just plays fast and loose with his insides day after day—you'd think he'd have more sense at his age. He'll come running in here at the last minute, stuff himself full of cold potatoes and biscuits and then go straight and get it bumped about from here to Balham. No wonder he spends a fortune on Rennies.

NELLIE. What do you want for sweet?

GRUNGE. What? (*He picks up a potato from the plate beside him*) Here, feel this. Cold as ice.

NELLIE. Give it here, I'll put it on the hot-plate.

(GRUNGE *rises, picks up his own dirty plate and the plate of dinner and takes them to the counter*)

GRUNGE. What's the good of warming up the bottom of the plate? He'll regret it when he's sixty-five. Slow suicide. Give us a packet of Weights. And a box of matches.

(NELLIE *serves Grunge with the cigarettes and matches.*
   NIMROD, *a driver, enters* R, *overcoated and with his collar turned up. He carries a vacuum flask*)

Cold out, Nim?

NIMROD (*moving to the table up* R) What the 'ell's the matter with you, then? (*He sits above the table up* R)

GRUNGE. Miserable old sod! (*He pays for the cigarettes and matches*)

NELLIE (*indicating the plate of food*) What you want me to do with this, then? (*She puts the money in the till*)

GRUNGE. It's as cold as it'll get. Fourteen minutes; I better go see if I can find him. Though, I don't see why I should bother. (*He crosses to the door* R) Not my stomach he's ruining. Put it in the oven.

(NIMROD *takes a packet of sandwiches from his pocket and unwraps them*)

NELLIE. It'll dry up.
GRUNGE. Let it.
NELLIE. What you want for sweet?
GRUNGE. What's in the fruit roll?
NELLIE. Fruit.
GRUNGE. What kind of fruit?
NELLIE. Dried fruit.

(NIMROD *eats his sandwiches*)

GRUNGE. Baked, you said?
NELLIE. Steamed.
GRUNGE. Custard?
NELLIE. Yes.
GRUNGE. Jam tart.

(GRUNGE *exits* R, *leaving the door open.*
NELLIE *exits to the kitchen with the dirty plate and the plate of food*)

NIMROD (*calling*) What about the door, then? (*He rises and closes the door*)

(*Before* NIMROD *has time to resume his seat, the door opens again and he pushes it.*
FRAN *enters* R *carrying a bucket, mop, brush and dust-pan*)

FRAN. Don't mind me, of course. (*She crosses to the counter, leaving the door open*)
NIMROD. What about the door, then?

. (FRAN *ignores Nimrod and puts her equipment down by the right end of the counter.* NIMROD *closes the door, resumes his seat and eats his sandwiches.*
NELLIE *enters from the kitchen*)

FRAN. I saw Sid last night.

NELLIE. He came to see you?

FRAN. Oh, no, he wouldn't do that.

NELLIE. You didn't go round and . . .

FRAN. No, no. It was by accident. In a pub.

NELLIE. I thought you didn't go to pubs.

FRAN. I was with my sister.

NELLIE. The married one?

FRAN. I only got one sister. She took me out to a pub for a drink last night; to cheer me up, she said. Me and her and Don.

NELLIE. Who's Don?

FRAN. Her husband. He's on the Underground. Anyway, we was at a table in the saloon, you see, and Marge had a . . .

NELLIE. Who's Marge?

FRAN. My *sister*. Marge had a gin and tonic and Don had a brown ale and I had a gin and lime, and there we was talking about her baby . . .

NELLIE. Whose?

FRAN. *Marge's.*

NELLIE. I thought she didn't have one.

FRAN. That's the one we was talking about. And then I happened to look up and there was Sid.

NELLIE. Where?

FRAN. At the next table.

NELLIE. By himself?

FRAN. "Don't look now, Marge," I said, "but look who's at the next table." And Don said, "Do you want to shift to the other bar?" But I said, "No, there's no need. I'm not doing him any harm sitting here, am I?"

(*A bus* INSPECTOR *enters* R, *sits* R *of the table* RC *and looks at the menu*)

NELLIE. Did he see you?

FRAN. Who—Sid? I dunno; he was fidgeting a bit. Anyway, after a bit I told Marge I thought I'd go over and say hallo to him. "What," she said, "you must be mad," she said, "after what he's done to you." And Don said, "You don't want to have no more truck with him, let's move to

the other bar," he said. "No," I said, "why should I?
After all, I only want to say hallo to him. There's no
harm in that."

NELLIE. They was right; you're a fool.

FRAN. "You'll make yourself cheap," says Marge.
"You've made yourself cheap enough already," she said.
And I said, "Well, if I have, I have; but if he owes me
nothing else, at least he owes me that," I said, "that he'll
say hallo to me at least. I can't see I'm making myself
cheap saying hallo to my husband," I said. So I got up
and went over to his table and I said, "Hallo, Sid."

(NIMROD *rises and crosses to the door* L)

NIMROD. Watch my sandwiches, will you?

NELLIE. Why, what they going to do?

(NIMROD *exits* L)

FRAN. You got any tea on the go, Nellie?

(NELLIE *pours a cup of tea for Fran*)

"Hallo, Sid," I said.

INSPECTOR (*calling*) Sausage toad.

NELLIE. There ain't any.

INSPECTOR. It says here "Sausage toad".

NELLIE. That was yesterday.

INSPECTOR. What's it doing on here, then?

NELLIE. You want the other side.

INSPECTOR. Other side of what?

NELLIE. Turn it round.

(*The* INSPECTOR *turns the card*)

Over—turn it over.

(*The* INSPECTOR *turns the card over*)

INSPECTOR. It's written upside down. (*He reverses the
card*) Ah! You want to cross it out if it's yesterday's.

NELLIE. It is crossed out.

INSPECTOR (*studying the card*) All *right*, then. Steak and
kidney pie.

NELLIE. None left.

INSPECTOR. What do you mean—"none left"?

NELLIE. I mean—none left. I can't help it if everyone wants steak and kidney pie.

INSPECTOR. You ought to foresee these things.

NELLIE. If you think you can do better, do the bleeding job yourself.

INSPECTOR. Don't you talk to me like that.

(NELLIE *comes from behind the counter and crosses to the Inspector*)

NELLIE. I've been back to the cardboard factory once, and I can go back again. Tomorrow. You keep a civil tongue in your head.

INSPECTOR. You'll hear about this.

NELLIE. What do you want to eat?

INSPECTOR. Haven't got much choice, have I?

NELLIE. No.

INSPECTOR. Give me the fish, then. And don't make the chips too big. I want small chips.

NELLIE. I'll sort 'em out for you.

(NELLIE *exits behind the counter.* FRAN *picks up her tea and sits* L *of the table up* R)

INSPECTOR. The Twenty-one's twenty minutes late, the Hundred and fourteen B's thirty-five minutes late, and the Six-four-two's disappeared off the face of the earth. What do they expect of me? We've got two drivers down with jaundice, one conductor with a dislocated toe and another one having a baby. It makes you sick. (*He indicates Fran's bucket*) Someone's going to trip over that lot in a minute.

(PUMFRET, *Grung's conductor, enters* R *and crosses to* C. FRAN *takes out a copy of the "Daily Mirror" and reads*)

(*To Pumfret*) We've lost a Six-four-two.

PUMFRET. Where's my dinner?

INSPECTOR. If it doesn't turn up before you leave, you'll have to turn round at Marshall's Corner, Pumfret.

PUMFRET. Where's Grunge? He was supposed to save me a dinner. (*He calls*) Nellie!

INSPECTOR. D'you hear what I say?

PUMFRET (*turning to the Inspector*) What?

INSPECTOR. I say since we've lost a Six-four-two . . .

PUMFRET. What do you mean—lost?

INSPECTOR. I don't know what I mean. It's gone.

PUMFRET. How can you lose a double-decker bus?

INSPECTOR. *I* haven't lost it.

PUMFRET. You're in charge, mate.

INSPECTOR. Now, look here . . .

PUMFRET. Where's my dinner? (*He calls*) Nellie!

(NELLIE *enters behind the counter with a plate of fish and chips. She collects cutlery, comes from the counter and puts the food on the table in front of the Inspector*)

NELLIE. Fish and chips.

PUMFRET. Where's my mate?

NELLIE. He's out looking for you. I don't know why you two can't never sit down together.

PUMFRET. I told him I'd be in.

INSPECTOR. Look at the size of these chips.

NELLIE. I picked out the smallest. They're French fried.

INSPECTOR. I don't care what country they are.

NELLIE. You provide the kitchen with a potato slicer and you'll get 'em the right size. I haven't time to go measuring them up.

INSPECTOR. All you've done is cut 'em in half.

NELLIE. French fried. (*To Pumfret*) Yours is in the oven, drying up.

(NELLIE *exits behind the counter*)

PUMFRET (*sitting above the left end of the table* RC) Grunge is like an old woman. He'll catch his death out there looking for me, the silly old fool. He's neurotic about time; fuss, fuss, fuss.

INSPECTOR. I wonder she bothers to cut 'em at all.

PUMFRET. Here, if we're going to turn round at Marshall's Corner, what about our cup of tea?

INSPECTOR. What cup of tea?

PUMFRET. The cup of tea we shan't have at the other end.

INSPECTOR. You can have a cup of tea when you get back.

PUMFRET. Back here? You mean we're to make two journeys without a break?

INSPECTOR. You'll get a break.

PUMFRET. Where?

INSPECTOR. Marshall's Corner.

PUMFRET. There's no caff there.

INSPECTOR. I told you, you can have your cup of tea when you've made the round trip.

PUMFRET. And make two journeys one after the other without a cup of tea.

INSPECTOR. Look, you're only going half-way.

PUMFRET. Don't tell me Marshall's Corner's half-way, it's more than half-way.

INSPECTOR. Marshall's Corner's *half-way*. Just over. Look at the times.

PUMFRET. Over half-way. You said it. That means there and back's more than our usual distance before we're entitled to a cup of tea. *Entitled.* Twice as much more.

INSPECTOR. What do you mean—"twice as much more"?

PUMFRET. There and back.

INSPECTOR (*taking out his notebook*) Here we are. (*He refers to the book*) Leave the garage—one-thirty-two, Marshall's Corner, two-fifty-six and you get to the other end four-fourteen.

PUMFRET. What does that make it?

(NELLIE *enters behind the counter with a plate of steak and kidney pie and potatoes and puts it in front of Pumfret*)

INSPECTOR. I'm trying to work it out.

PUMFRET (*looking at his meal*) Looks a bit dry, don't it?

NELLIE. If you don't like it, you know what you can do. I'm not a slave to this establishment.

PUMFRET. Service with a smile.

(NELLIE *exits behind the counter*)

INSPECTOR. One hour twenty-four minutes.

PUMFRET. Where to?

INSPECTOR. Marshall's Corner.

PUMFRET. And what is it from there?

INSPECTOR. You're not going any farther.

PUMFRET. I just want to know.

INSPECTOR. One hour eighteen.

PUMFRET. There you are.

INSPECTOR. What?

PUMFRET. Six minutes difference.

INSPECTOR. Six minutes won't kill you, will it?

PUMFRET. Six minutes is all right. But this is twelve. There and back. The journey's too long as it is, you know that as well as I do.

INSPECTOR. But you'll have a *break* half-way.

PUMFRET. More than half-way.

INSPECTOR. Half-way.

PUMFRET. There's six minutes . . .

INSPECTOR. Half-way there and back.

PUMFRET. Without a cup of tea. And what happens if I want to go to the lav? There's nothing at Marshall's Corner.

INSPECTOR. There never has been.

PUMFRET. Well, then!

INSPECTOR. Well then, you can do what you usually do.

PUMFRET. I usually wait till the other end.

INSPECTOR. Then you can wait till you get back here, can't you? And have it with your tea.

PUMFRET. You expect me to hang on for an extra twelve minutes?

INSPECTOR. Six minutes.

PUMFRET. Twelve! There and back.

INSPECTOR. But you don't want to go till you get there.

PUMFRET. How do you know when I'll want to go? (*He pauses*) This is sheer regimentation.

INSPECTOR. You know what you're being, you're being obstructionist.

PUMFRET. Oh, really!

INSPECTOR. I've had buses turn round at Marshall's Corner time after time before now. And nothing said.

PUMFRET. Ah, but you forget one thing. Times have

changed. Bus crews are in short supply. The old days are gone, mate. We don't strain our bladders for anyone.

(*There is a pause*)

INSPECTOR. All right, then. All right, then. We know where we stand.
PUMFRET. That's right.

(*There is a pause. They eat*)

Mind *you*, if you want a help out, I don't mind turning round at Marshall's Corner.

(*The* INSPECTOR *lowers his fork*)

After all, we're all in it together, aren't we, mate? 'Course, I can't speak for my driver; Grunge isn't easy like me. I suppose I'd better hurry up and find him. Tell him to stop looking for me. (*He takes a potato*)
INSPECTOR. Here!
PUMFRET. What's up?
INSPECTOR. What's that on your plate?
PUMFRET. I dunno. Looks like steak and kidney pie. I only eat the potatoes.

(*The* INSPECTOR *rises and goes to the counter*)

INSPECTOR (*calling*) Nellie.

(NELLIE *enters behind the counter*)

NELLIE. What?
INSPECTOR. I thought you said the pie was finished. (*He points to Pumfret's plate*) What's that over there, then?
NELLIE. That's the last of it.
INSPECTOR. But he came in after me.
NELLIE. It was ordered.
INSPECTOR. He's not even eating it.
NELLIE. Then what are you complaining about? Anything else?
INSPECTOR. Give us a cup of tea.

(NELLIE *pours a cup of tea for the Inspector*)

(*He casts around and sees Fran*) Are you supposed to be sweeping up, or aren't you?

(FRAN *finishes her tea, rises, collects her broom and begins to sweep.* PUMFRET *rises, picks up his plate, moves and puts it on the counter*)

PUMFRET. Can't eat any more of that. Give us a couple of packets of biscuits, Nell. And some Rennies.

NELLIE. Setlers.

PUMFRET. They'll do. All grist to the mill. (*He puts a ten-shilling note on the counter*) Take it out of that.

(NELLIE *quickly serves Pumfret with the biscuits and Setlers, puts the note in the till and gives him his change, then exits behind the counter*)

INSPECTOR. Why have it if you don't want it? There's other people . . .

(FRAN *stops sweeping and watches*)

PUMFRET. I like the gravy. If Grunge comes in, I'm looking for him. (*He crosses to the door* R)

INSPECTOR. Sheer criminal waste. Don't forget about Marshall's Corner, then.

(PUMFRET *stops, turns and moves to the Inspector*)

PUMFRET. Time was when bus crews did what they was told and no questions asked. We was ten a penny, see? But times have changed; we're on top, now.

INSPECTOR. Well?

PUMFRET. That's why we can afford to be magnanimous —as long as no-one thinks it's creating a precedent. Don't *you* forget *that*.

(PUMFRET *exits* R, *singing*)

INSPECTOR (*rounding on Fran*) What do you think you're gawping at? (*He picks up his tea and resumes his seat at the table* RC)

(FRAN *crosses and sweeps down* L.

GIMLET, *a driver, and* LILLIAN, *his conductress, enter* R. LILLIAN *carries her handbag and a book.* GIMLET *removes his*

B

coat and cap. LILLIAN *crosses and is about to put her bag and
book on the chair below the left end of the table* RC, *but* GIMLET
forestalls her and flings his coat and cap on the chair. LILLIAN
moves and puts her book and bag on the chair L *of the table
up* R)

(*He looks at his watch. To Gimlet*) Well, at least *you're* on
time.

GIMLET. I'm always on time. What are you getting at?

INSPECTOR. All I said . . .

GIMLET. Have you ever known me not on time? You
want to make a complaint?

INSPECTOR. Now, look here . . .

GIMLET. Though I tell you this: if I *was* late in today,
I'd have every excuse. I've had nothing but obstruction,
obstruction, from first to last.

LILLIAN (*moving above the table* RC) If you mean by obstruction a few old ladies waiting at request stops, that you
couldn't bother to pull up for . . .

GIMLET (*sitting* L *of the table* RC) She wasn't waiting at a
request stop, she was on the other side of the road.

LILLIAN. She was half-way across and waving her umbrella. It was quite obvious she wanted to get on.

(FRAN *stops sweeping and listens*)

GIMLET. Oh, get lost!

LILLIAN. Poor old lady; to leave her standing there in the
cold . . .

GIMLET. She wasn't old! She was middle-bloody-aged!

LILLIAN. How do you know? We went past at forty
miles an hour.

GIMLET. Am I to stop every time some old dear waves an
umbrella in the distance?

LILLIAN. I think it's disgusting. We are the servants of
the public.

GIMLET. Wrap up, will you? Let's have a rest from each
other for half an hour.

LILLIAN (*moving to the door* R) As for *why* you're so keen to
be back on time—we all know the reason for that.

(LILLIAN *exits* R)

GIMLET. Why don't you drop dead!

(*But the door has closed behind her*)

INSPECTOR. What's this, then?

GIMLET (*calling*) Nellie! (*To Fran*) Where is that woman?

FRAN. She's gone.

GIMLET. I want something to eat.

FRAN. She's having her lunch.

GIMLET. And what am I supposed to do?

(FRAN *puts down her broom and goes behind the counter*)

FRAN. Fish and chips or pie?

NELLIE (*off; calling*) There's no pie.

FRAN. There's no pie. Fish and chips or nothing.

GIMLET. All right, then.

FRAN. All right—what?

GIMLET. All right—fish and chips.

(FRAN *exits behind the counter*)

INSPECTOR. They're not chips, neither. They're boiled potatoes cut in half and dropped into lukewarm fat.

GIMLET. I don't care what I eat. Got no appetite, anyway.

INSPECTOR. What's all this about request stops, then? And forty mile an hour?

GIMLET. I want to change my conductor. I've had enough, do you hear? I don't care who I go out with, but I'm not going out again with that woman. I don't know what it is but every time she rings the bell I feel like running the bus through a shop window. We're incompatible.

INSPECTOR. Have you been ignoring request stops, or haven't you?

GIMLET. If anyone wants to lay a complaint let 'em lay a complaint.

INSPECTOR. Speeding's a serious offence.

GIMLET. I wish someone would. You hear that? I wish someone would get me the sack so I could scrape the dust of this concern off my feet and get back to making doughnuts again.

INSPECTOR. Nobody's keeping you here against your will. If you don't like the job . . .

GIMLET. All right, all right. (*He pauses*) I didn't see the Six-four-two when I came in.

INSPECTOR. No.

GIMLET. Should have been in twenty minutes ago.

INSPECTOR. That's right.

GIMLET. Can't have gone out again.

INSPECTOR. No.

GIMLET. Well?

INSPECTOR. Hasn't been in.

GIMLET. Twenty minutes late?

INSPECTOR. Twenty-two and a half.

GIMLET. How's that, then?

INSPECTOR. That's right.

GIMLET. I said, "How's that, then"?

INSPECTOR. I dunno. (*He eats stolidly*)

GIMLET. Don't give me a clue, will you?

INSPECTOR. Why do you want to know? Want to take my job over?

GIMLET. But it's the quietest service in the district.

INSPECTOR. That's right.

GIMLET. And a straight road all the way from Marshall's Corner.

INSPECTOR. That's right.

GIMLET. So he's broken it down, has he?

INSPECTOR. Who?

GIMLET. Dogg. Bert Dogg, the bloke who calls himself the driver. He's done it on purpose.

INSPECTOR. Who done what?

GIMLET. What did he give it—a puncture?

INSPECTOR. Pass the vinegar.

GIMLET. Was it?

INSPECTOR. Pass the vinegar.

(GIMLET *passes the vinegar*)

'Tasn't broken down.

GIMLET. What, then?

INSPECTOR. It's gone.

GIMLET. What do you mean—gone?

INSPECTOR. Gone.

GIMLET. For the love of Mike . . .

INSPECTOR. Disappeared. It's not on the rout.

GIMLET. You've lost a double-decker bus!

INSPECTOR. Now, look here, I've had enough of this. You all think I've got a cushy number, don't you? I know what's said about me behind my back. Well, just you try my job for a change, that's all. Go on, try it. Here, take me cap. And here's me book. You go and see if you can do better. I tell you, there's nothing but grouse, grouse on this job from the lot of you, crews, passengers, the lot—grouse, grouse, grouse. You grouse if I change the time-tables and if I leave things as they are you still grouse. I'm sick of the lot of you; you're nothing but a lot of—of—of left-wingers.

GIMLET. Don't you call me a left-winger.

INSPECTOR. What else are you, then, eh, what else?

GIMLET. My union'll hear about this.

INSPECTOR. Take my book, go on, take it.

GIMLET. I don't want your blasted book!

(*There is a pause. The* INSPECTOR *and* GIMLET *look murderously at each other, then both rise and move silently to the counter.*

FRAN *enters behind the counter*)

(*To Fran*) Where's my bleeding dinner?

FRAN. There wasn't no more chips. Nellie just had the last of 'em.

GIMLET. So what am I supposed to do?

FRAN. Wait ten minutes.

(GIMLET *crosses and wanders out* R)

INSPECTOR. Tomato sauce.

FRAN. O.K. (*She passes him a bottle of O.K. sauce from the shelves behind her*)

INSPECTOR. I said "tomato".

FRAN. O.K. We've only got O.K., I'm telling you.

INSPECTOR. All right.

FRAN. O.K.

(FRAN *exits behind the counter.*
GRUNGE *enters* R *and crosses to* C)

GRUNGE. I can't find my conductor.

INSPECTOR. He's out looking for you.

GRUNGE. It's like a bloody merry-go-round. (*He crosses to the door* R)

INSPECTOR. I want you to turn round at Marshall's Corner this trip, Grunge.

(GRUNGE *stops and turns*)

GRUNGE. What about our cup of tea?

INSPECTOR. See Pumfret about it.

(GRUNGE *exits* R. *The* INSPECTOR *resumes his seat* R *of the table* RC *and pours sauce on his meal as though emptying it down a sink.*
GIMLET *enters* R)

GIMLET (*crossing and sitting* L *of the table* RC) No sign of it.

INSPECTOR. What?

GIMLET. The bus.

INSPECTOR. 'Tain't your worry. (*He pauses*) It wasn't always like this.

GIMLET. Like what?

INSPECTOR. Like it is now.

GIMLET. I wouldn't know.

INSPECTOR. Well, I'm telling you. It wasn't always like this. Once they was dedicated men.

GIMLET. Go on!

INSPECTOR. In nineteen-thirty-eight there was a driver, name of Hackett, was climbing into his cab at the change-over at Parson's Green when he slipped and fractured the big toe on his left foot. What d'you think he did?

GIMLET. Fractured the big toe on his . . .

INSPECTOR. All right, listen: he drove that bus all the way back to the depot, though every change of gear was sheer agony. Turned up dead on schedule. "The bus had to get through," he said. Dedication.

GIMLET. What did he get out of it?

INSPECTOR. He was highly commended.

GIMLET. How much is that in pounds?

INSPECTOR. Strike a light! You blokes today . . .

GIMLET. I'm not going to argue the toss about it. (*He pauses*) So he's taken the bus, has he? That's going a bit far.

INSPECTOR. Who?

GIMLET. Bert Dogg, of course. Taken her off in a double-decker bus.

INSPECTOR. What's it to do with you, anyway?

GIMLET. As a matter of fact, I had something to say to a member of the crew.

INSPECTOR. Not Dogg, I take it.

GIMLET. I've nothing to say to Dogg. Him and me don't speak the same language.

INSPECTOR. Ho, ho, I see.

GIMLET. I've only got half an hour; he knows that, of course. He's checked up. Or they've put him on to it.

INSPECTOR. Who's "they"?

GIMLET. Them. You realize, I suppose, that this is no accident. He was destined to run off with that bus; it was in the *stars*.

INSPECTOR. Are you mad?

GIMLET. Maybe I am at that. I tell you this: I'm sick of this job. I've had enough of it, the lot. End of the week I get me cards. I don't give a bugger if the bus comes in or not. (*He rises*) Think I'll go down to the office and see if there's any word. (*He crosses to the door* R)

INSPECTOR. That's what I like to see. Dedication.

(GIMLET *exits* R, *slamming the door behind him. There is a pause.*

FRAN *enters behind the counter and stands above the table* RC)

FRAN. I saw Sid last night.

INSPECTOR. What?

FRAN. I saw Sid last night.

INSPECTOR. What's for sweet?

FRAN (*indicating the menu*) It's writ on there.

(*The* INSPECTOR *picks up the menu and looks at it*)

INSPECTOR. Syrup pudding. Only I don't want any syrup with it. You get me? I just want the pudding. Middle cut. I don't want an end piece. (*Sarcastically*) You think you can do that?

FRAN. No.

INSPECTOR. Why not?

FRAN. You got the wrong side of the menu again.

(*There is a pause. The* INSPECTOR *turns the menu over*)

INSPECTOR. Fruit roll, then.

FRAN. Off.

INSPECTOR. Now, look here . . .

FRAN. Nellie's just had the last piece. I can't call it back, can I?

INSPECTOR. Bring me the jam tart.

(FRAN *picks up the Inspector's empty plate and moves behind the counter*)

Without custard.

FRAN. I'm not sure we got any without custard. We got some custard without tart.

(FRAN *exits behind the counter.*

NIMROD *enters* R, *sits at his table up* R *and eats his sandwiches*)

NIMROD. Cold out there. We're in for some slush soon.

INSPECTOR (*rising, moving to* L *of the table up* R *and facing Nimrod*) You mean snow?

NIMROD. It turns to slush, don't it? Let's not kid ourselves. All this Christmas card stuff. If I had my way, you know what Christmas cards would have on them? Slush.

(LILLIAN *enters* R, *closes the door and crosses to the counter*)

(*Without looking up from his sandwiches*) What about the door, then?

LILLIAN. It happens to be closed.

NIMROD (*to the Inspector*) Sky's like porridge. Sleet sky, that's what that is. And tonight it'll freeze. Be murder on the roads in the morning. And that east wind goes right through you.

INSPECTOR. Last summer you was complaining about the heat.

NIMROD. We didn't have any summer.

INSPECTOR. You was complaining about it, all the same. Trouble with you, you don't eat proper food. What good are sandwiches? You want a hot meal.

NIMROD. I get a hot meal at home.

INSPECTOR. Want to get something hot down you, mid-day. Have some fish and chips.

NIMROD. Don't like fish and chips. I only like sausage and mash.

INSPECTOR. How can you only like sausage and mash?

NIMROD. No law against it, is there?

INSPECTOR. You mean to say you never eat nothing else?

NIMROD. Why should I? I don't like anything else.

INSPECTOR. Every day you have . . . ?

NIMROD. Do you mind!

INSPECTOR. What does your wife think about that?

NIMROD. What she thinks is her business. She used to try it on, once upon a time. Used to cook fancy stuff, veal cutlets and muck, but I soon put a stop to that. "You can put this back where it came from," I said to her, "you know what I like and that's what I'm going to get, from now on, and none of your half-larks," I said. "What," she said, "every day?" "Yes," I said, "why not? If I like it why shouldn't I have it every day?" "You'll get sick of it," she said. "Now, look here," I said, "when I get sick of it I'll say so. Until then," I said, "I'm going to have it. Every day." "And what about me?" she said. "What do you mean, 'what about you?'" I said. "I mean, am I to have no say in it?" she said. "Say?" I said. "Yes," she said, "do you expect me to have it every day whether I want it or not?" "What's the matter," I said, "don't you like it?" "Not every day," she said. "Well, listen here," I said, "you better get this straight. I want it every day and I'm going to have it every day, and if I don't get it from you I'll get it from someone else." "What do you mean by that?" she said. "Fred's caff," I said, "that's what I mean. I can get it from Fred's caff any day of the week. I know the girl behind the counter."

INSPECTOR. What about Christmas?

NIMROD. What about it? Not my fault, is it?

INSPECTOR. You have sausage and mash at Christmas?

NIMROD. Why not? Stick a bit of holly in it.

LILLIAN (*calling*) Am I to have any service?

(FRAN *enters behind the counter*)

FRAN. Fish and chips.

LILLIAN. Or what?

FRAN. Or nothing.

LILLIAN. What sort of fish is it?

FRAN. Fried fish.

LILLIAN. Fried what?

FRAN. Fish.

LILLIAN. But *what*? Plaice, cod, haddock?

FRAN. You mean—before it was fried?

LILLIAN. It doesn't matter.

FRAN. Nellie might have known. (*She calls*) Nellie!

(*There is no answer*)

No answer.

LILLIAN. It doesn't *matter*.

FRAN. Fish and chips, then. It'll be five minutes.

(FRAN *exits behind the counter*)

LILLIAN. I wonder why everything has to be so—shabby.
Dismal. Temporary. I'm sure it's quite unnecessary. This
should be an age of consummation, full of light and grace.
Here we are, past the middle of the twentieth century.
With all that implies. The prospects are unlimited. And
what comes out of it. Fish and chips or nothing. Sauce
bottles congealed at the top. Zinc alloy forks with twisted
prongs. Rubber bread. Plastic tablecloths. Who could
have imagined it, fifty years ago? "What?" I can hear
them saying, "With atomic energy and humanism? All
will be light and air and cultured ease." Not that I'm complaining. On the contrary; complaining, or rather the
attitude of mind that goes with it, is the cause of all the
trouble. If people complained less they'd have more time
to open their eyes to what we have and what we need;

what we have and should be thankful for, and what we need and should work for. We need a positive attitude, we need joy. Though where it's to come from it's hard to say.

NIMROD. You talking to me?

LILLIAN. To no-one in particular.

NIMROD. You want to wait till you get to my age, my girl. Then you'll see.

LILLIAN. See what? What'll I see?

NIMROD. Nothing.

INSPECTOR. Atomic energy's one thing, bus time-tables are another. (*He turns to the counter and calls*) Fran!

(FRAN *enters behind the counter*)

Where's my jam tart, then?

FRAN. Ooh, I forgot.

(FRAN *exits behind the counter. The* INSPECTOR *resumes his seat* R *of the table* RC)

LILLIAN. On the contrary . . .

INSPECTOR. What?

LILLIAN. (*moving to* L *of the table* RC) On the contrary, they're both part of the twentieth century. Why should one be up to date and the other archaic?

INSPECTOR. Now, look here . . .

LILLIAN. It's absolutely ridiculous. Little men in long overcoats standing on street corners with their little time-tables—stagecoach technique pure and simple. And what happens? You lose buses.

INSPECTOR. Now, look here . . .

LILLIAN. You see, all you can ever say is "look here". You've no defence for the system.

INSPECTOR. I suppose you think it's a cushy job standing on street corners?

LILLIAN. You miss the point.

INSPECTOR. You want to try it, that's all, just try it. Go out there in the drizzle and try it.

LILLIAN. That isn't the *point*.

INSPECTOR. Ah! No! You'd say "point" if you was out there with frozen fingers. You'd talk about "point".

LILLIAN. Oh, dear, oh, dear.

INSPECTOR. You'd say "oh, dear, oh, dear," if you was out there.

LILLIAN. "Nothing but misery all around I see . . ."

INSPECTOR. You'd see it if you was out there. Where's my sweet, then?

(FRAN *enters behind the counter with a plate of jam tart and custard and collects a spoon and fork*)

NIMROD. There's no joy in any of it.

LILLIAN. That depends on the person, if I may say so.

NIMROD. All right, just wait. Twenty years, that's all, just twenty years.

(FRAN *puts the sweet in front of the Inspector*)

LILLIAN. Wait for what?

NIMROD. You'll see.

INSPECTOR. What's this, then? I said "no custard".

FRAN. I couldn't take it off once it's on, could I? It's all soaked in.

(FRAN *moves behind the counter.* NIMROD *screws the top on his vacuum flask, folds up and pockets his wrappers, and rises*)

NIMROD (*moving to the counter*) Light and *what*? (*To Fran*) Ten Woods. (*To Lillian*) Grace? Light and grace?

(FRAN *serves* NIMROD *with the cigarettes. He puts down the money and waits for the change.* FRAN *puts the money in the till and the change on the counter*)

(*To Lillian*) Not married, are you?

LILLIAN. That has nothing to do with it. (*She moves and sits* L *of the table up* R)

NIMROD. Ha, ha! (*He picks up his change, moves to Lillian, fishes his wallet out of an inside pocket, opens it, pulls out a photograph and shows it to her*) Look at that.

LILLIAN. What is it?

NIMROD. Me. Nineteen-thirty-five. Taken on Beachy Head. Member of the Socialist Party, I was. Didn't believe in money. Everything was going to be fine. I was just waiting for the day. (*He replaces the photograph and wallet in his pocket*)

LILLIAN. You've missed the point.

(NIMROD *crosses to the door* R *then stops and turns*)

NIMROD. What point? What the hell point?

(NIMROD *exits* R. LILLIAN *opens her book*)

INSPECTOR. He don't eat properly. That's his trouble.

(FRAN *enters behind the counter with a plate of fish and chips. She collects cutlery and puts the meal on the table in front of Lillian*)

FRAN. Fish and chips.
LILLIAN. Thank you.

(FRAN *sits above the table up* R)

FRAN. Did I ever tell you about Sid?
LILLIAN. Yes.
FRAN. Well, I saw him last night.
LILLIAN. Really?
FRAN. In a pub. I was with my sister Marge and her husband. And I happened to look up and there he was.
LILLIAN (*after a pause*) Who?
FRAN. Sid. Only he didn't see me, or anyway he kept his eyes away. He was with someone else, you see. No-one I knew. She may not even have known about me. I mean, he could have kept quiet about it. After all, he might not want to have to go explaining how things are every time he meets someone. Not at first, anyway. Just as well to keep it dark, perhaps.
LILLIAN. You're too easy.
FRAN. That's what Marge says, but I don't see it. Anyway, I thought I'd go over and say hallo to him.
LILLIAN. After what he's done to you?
FRAN. He didn't do nothing to me. Only left me. It's a free country. (*She pauses*) After all, he must have wanted to.
LILLIAN. What?
FRAN. Leave me. To *leave* me. You can't help what you want, can you? I wouldn't like to think of his staying on with me if he didn't want to.

LILLIAN. Why not, if it's his duty?

FRAN. I don't know nothing about duty. So, as I say, I thought I'd go up and say hallo to him.

LILLIAN (*after a pause*) Well?

FRAN. So I did.

INSPECTOR. Cup of tea.

FRAN (*rising*) I went across to where he was sitting with this friend, and I stood there and he still didn't see me, or at least he didn't seem to, and I said: "Hallo, Sid," I said.

INSPECTOR. With sugar.

(FRAN *collects the Inspector's empty plate, goes behind the counter and pours a cup of tea.*
PUMFRET *enters* R)

PUMFRET (*crossing to* C) Well, here we are again.

INSPECTOR. Pumfret! What the devil are you doing here? Why aren't you on the rout?

PUMFRET. It was coming on to rain, so we decided not to go.

INSPECTOR. Have you gone mad?

PUMFRET. Keep your hair on; it was an act of God.

INSPECTOR. What are you talking about?

PUMFRET. He gave us a flat tyre.

INSPECTOR. Good Lord!

PUMFRET. I left Grunge at the helm while they change the wheel. Grunge never deserts a sinking ship. Cup of tea, please, Fran.

INSPECTOR. It all just transpires against me, that's what it does. Transpires. (*He rises and moves to the door* R)

FRAN. What about your tea?

PUMFRET. It's all right. I'll drink it.

(GIMLET *enters* R)

GIMLET. There's no word of that bus.

INSPECTOR. What do you expect me to do about it?

(*The* INSPECTOR *exits* R.
FRAN *exits behind the counter.* PRUMFRET *picks up the cup of tea and sits above the left end of the table* RC)

GIMLET. 'Course it's nothing to do with you if a bus vanishes into thin air. How I hate that bloke.

LILLIAN. Is there anyone you don't hate?

(GIMLET *glares balefully at Lillian and crosses to the counter*)

Bus inspectors; old ladies at request stops . . .

GIMLET. If you think I'm spending my dinner break arguing the toss with you, you're wrong.

LILLIAN. You hate everybody. Even yourself, I dare say. Not that I'd blame you for that.

GIMLET. Put another record on. (*He paces up and down* L)

(FRAN *enters behind the counter with a plate of fish and chips, which she puts on the counter*)

(*He looks at his watch*) My last chance for a fortnight. Oh, he's clever, is Dogg. I could wring his neck. The feeling of having his throat between my fingers . . .

FRAN. Don't you want your dinner?

GIMLET. What?

FRAN. Your fish.

GIMLET (*moving to the counter*) All right, give it here. Suppose I'd better eat it. (*He collects the food and some cutlery and sits morosely* L *of the table* RC, *but does not eat*)

PUMFRET. Life goes on, mate.

GIMLET. Hm!

PUMFRET. Sometimes it gets worse and sometimes it don't.

GIMLET. When I want philosophy I'll ask you for it.

PUMFRET. That's not philosophy, it's fact. The fruit of my experience. When you get to my age . . .

GIMLET. With any luck I shan't, shall I? (*He pauses*) You want my dinner?

PUMFRET. Don't you want it?

GIMLET. I wouldn't give it away if I did, would I?

PUMFRET. You worried about the H-bomb?

GIMLET. Bugger the H-bomb!

PUMFRET. I thought you weren't. Love, eh?

GIMLET. What are you talking about?

PUMFRET. I'll just have some of the batter. (*He helps himself*)

GIMLET (*looking at his watch*) Nineteen minutes left.

PUMFRET. I was that way once. She worked in a tobacconist's. Her name was Peggy. It was terrible; I couldn't sleep, had no appetite. It's a funny business. Unreasonable you know. Look at this. (*He takes out a photograph and shows it to Gimlet*) Well?

GIMLET. Well—what?

PUMFRET. That was Peggy.

GIMLET. What am I supposed to do?

PUMFRET. What do you think of her?

GIMLET. Nothing.

PUMFRET. You've hit the nail on the head. That's just the way I feel. I look at this photo and I think, "Well, there's a fine example of nothing at all."

LILLIAN (*to Fran*) May I have a cup of coffee, please?

(FRAN *pours a cup of coffee for Lillian*)

PUMFRET. Mind *you*, *that* was nearly ten years ago. She had me, then. For six months she had me. I was so taken up with her I even introduced her to my wife. (*He takes out another photograph*) There they both are—side by side. That's our back garden. We had a nice show of wallflowers that year. We used to play rummy together, the three of us. And then one day I suddenly realized I was getting more of a kick out of the rummy than I was from Peggy. So that was that.

(FRAN *takes the coffee to Lillian then returns behind the counter*)

GIMLET. Then why carry her photo about?

PUMFRET. To remind me. Whenever I see something that takes my fancy, I take this out and look at it and I say to myself, "Don't kid yourself, mate. Give her six months and this'll be her—a wonderful example of absolutely nothing." (*He pockets the photographs and helps himself to more batter*) Looks sort of naked with its batter off, don't it?

(GIMLET *rises and goes to the counter*)

GIMLET (*to Fran*) Give us a cup of tea.

FRAN. I saw Sid last night.

GIMLET. Oh, for the love of Mike! (*He moves down* L)

(FRAN *pours a cup of tea*)

LILLIAN. Boor. Boor.

GIMLET (*turning to Lillian*) Look, in something over quarter of an hour we've got to share the same bus. Meanwhile, perhaps you could keep out of my hair. I'm sick, sick, sick of this. (*He goes to the pin-table and puts a penny in*)

FRAN. D'you want your tea?

GIMLET. No.

LILLIAN (*quietly*) Boor. Boor.

(GIMLET *slams the pin-table. The "tilt" sign lights up*)

GIMLET. Sod all pin-tables! (*He turns away and resumes his seat* L *of the table* RC. *To Pumfret*) You've got it all wrong, mate.

PUMFRET. What?

GIMLET. About this girl.

PUMFRET (*rising*) I'll have that tea if you don't want it. (*He collects the cup of tea from the counter and resumes his seat*)

GIMLET. I can get women any day of the week. Look, I've got three on the go at *present*.

(PUMFRET *drinks his tea*)

You ever worked in a bakery?

PUMFRET. No.

GIMLET. I was apprenticed. My old man's idea. "Whatever happens," he said, "there'll always be bread. You work hard," he used to say, "keep your nose clean, don't sauce your superiors, do as you're told and never do nothing anyone can take exception to. And if it's ever a choice between shining like a star and being ordinary, you be dead ordinary," he said. "And in ten years you'll have a nice steady job with a nice steady wage and no-one can touch you." Six years I had of long tins and small tins and coburgs and Vienna rotten twists. I stuck it. Then they put me on doughnuts. All night long I used to turn out doughnuts. I stank of doughnuts. I had three weeks of it and then I went to the boss. "What's the matter?" he says, "Don't you like making doughnuts?" "How can you *like* making doughnuts?" I said, "How can anyone like making doughnuts? What do you take me for," I said, "a cretin? You think I'm like the rest of them in there?" I said, "Because I'll tell you what they are, they're a bunch of bloody nitwits. Just tell me this," I said, "perhaps I'm missing something, maybe I'm stupid; but what am I supposed to be getting out of making doughnuts for you?" "There's plenty to take the job over if you don't want it," he said. "Is there? Right. Fine. In that case", I said, "you can do you-know-what with your bakehouse and your doughnuts, as well, one by one, because I'm getting out from under." I lost my temper, see? I'd had enough.

(LILLIAN *finishes her meal, rises, goes to the counter and pays Fran*)

LILLIAN. I'm going for a walk.

GIMLET. What am I supposed to do? Chase you?

LILLIAN. It's immaterial to me.

(LILLIAN *exits* R)

FRAN (*putting the money in the till*) In that case, I suppose I can have my dinner. Nellie'll be finished.

(FRAN *exits behind the counter*)

GIMLET. Do you ever have a feeling you're being got at?

PUMFRET. Who by?

GIMLET. How do I know? *Them.* Things keep getting in your hair. Whatever you try to do goes sour on you.

PUMFRET. Why you, specially?

GIMLET. I don't know. There's blokes worked in that bakehouse year in year out, living so ordinary you could scream. Yet they never feel they've been got at. Well, then, if I'm not being got at who's getting at me to make me feel I *am* being got at? I tell you, sometimes I just want to find something to take a sock at.

PUMFRET. It's love, mate. It mixes things up.

GIMLET. I tell you it's not love. You've got it all wrong. Look, I took Iris out a couple of times not long after I started at this job. The pictures and that. She's a nice kid in her way, and I don't like going to the pictures on my own, especially when they're crummy as they usually are. All right, and then the next time I want to take her to some crummy film she's had her schedule changed, so I can't. So be it, it's no skin off my nose, except I don't like having my plans mucked up, see? So I try to arrange some other time. And I find whenever I'm working early she's working late, and when she's working early *I'm* working late. This irritates me, you see; it don't matter, but it *irritates* me. Well, we finally coincide again, and on the night I'm to go out with her her mother gets taken bad at Woking and she takes a fortnight off to look after her. You can't blame her for that, can you? I hang on till she comes back, and then I try to bump into her at the depot so I can arrange to take her to the pictures. Only we never quite seem to get to the depot at the same time. And when I finally do see her, she's working late again and I'm working early. Meanwhile, I find she's being taken out by this bloke Dogg, and if there's any one I can't stand it's this bloke *Dogg*.

PUMFRET. Why?

GIMLET. I don't know. I've nothing against him. I just hate his guts. No reason why he shouldn't take her out, it makes no odds to me. It's just a bit galling not to be able to do a simple thing like take a girl you don't even much care about to the *pictures*. So I find I'm spending all my time looking up bus times and cinema times like Napoleon planning a battle and I'm even less satisfied with my lot than I was at the doughnuts. So I tell myself I'll have one last go and if I find I'm still being got at I'll cut my losses and go back to baking. On consulting my charts I find we're both due in together today, that is now, we're both off early tomorrow night, and the local cinema hasn't up to the present moment either blown up or burnt down. So I make it my business to get in on schedule, in spite of sundry old dears with tortoise disease who've been planted at request stops all along the route so as to flag me down with their umbrellas and then change their minds when I've stopped. And in spite of a certain female conductress who likes to give the passengers time to settle down and take off their shoes and admire the scenery before she deigns to ring the bell. And when I get here against all the odds,

what do I find? Only that that—bastard Dogg—has taken
his bus together with Iris and gone off on holiday with it.
I'd fixed everything else, you see. But I hadn't thought of
him taking the bus and all.

(*There is a pause.* PUMFRET *rises, moves* LC *and stands
looking at Gimlet for a few moments*)

PUMFRET. You was born under the wrong star, mate.

(PUMFRET *crosses and exits* R.
    NELLIE *enters behind the counter and busies herself collecting
the dirty plates, etc., and putting them on the counter*)

NELLIE (*collecting Gimlet's plate*) You made a right mess of
this fish, haven't you? Waste of good protein, that is.

GIMLET. It hasn't been touched. Put more batter round
it.

(*The* INSPECTOR *enters* R)

INSPECTOR (*moving above the table* RC) I've found where
it is.

GIMLET. You don't say!

INSPECTOR. Don't you want to know?

GIMLET. What the hell's it to me?

(*The* INSPECTOR *turns away*)

All right, where is it, then?

(GRUNGE *enters* R)

GRUNGE. I've lost my mate again.

INSPECTOR. Haven't you gone, yet?

GRUNGE. I've been sitting there freezing. We've had the
wheel on five minutes ago. Can't go with no conductor,
can I?

INSPECTOR. Look in the lav.

GRUNGE. You'd think he was avoiding me.

(GRUNGE *exits* R)

INSPECTOR. All the spirit's gone out of public transport.
No *esprit de corpse* nowadays. Might as well all wrap up and
go home.

GIMLET. Where is it?

INSPECTOR. You know Dogg used to be on the number Fourteens? Single-decker route—turns off right at Marshall's Corner.

(PUMFRET *enters* R)

PUMFRET. That wheel done, yet?
INSPECTOR. It's been on five minutes. Your driver's looking for you.
PUMFRET. I'm off, then. If he comes in again—I've gone.

(PUMFRET *exits* R)

INSPECTOR. It has to be a single-decker rout, you see, for the simple reason is, there's a low bridge across the road. Barely fourteen foot headroom. Well, it seems Dogg had a lapse of memory today.
GIMLET. What!
INSPECTOR. Yes. He turned right at Marshall's Corner.
GIMLET. What lengths won't they go to get at me!
INSPECTOR. I don't know what you're talking about.
GIMLET. *They* know, though. *They* know.

(GRUNGE *enters* R)

GRUNGE. Can't find him.
INSPECTOR. He's gone.
GRUNGE. Oh, blimey! I ought to get double time on this job. (*He turns to go*)
NELLIE. What about your jam tart?
GRUNGE. What jam tart?
NELLIE. You ordered jam tart.
GRUNGE. That was my mate.
NELLIE. It was you.
GRUNGE. Then I don't want it.
NELLIE. You're not going to let it go to waste!
GRUNGE. All right, wrap it up. I'll take it with me.
NELLIE. With custard on it?
GRUNGE. Oh, I dunno.

(GRUNGE *exits* R)

GIMLET. Was anyone hurt?

INSPECTOR. Nothing serious. Only now, of course, we've got our first open-top double-decker.

(*The* INSPECTOR *exits* R. GIMLET *rises, goes to the pin-table and begins to play*)

NELLIE. You'll never win. It's not made so's you can win.

GIMLET (*looking at Nellie*) Some people could.

(IRIS, *Dogg's conductress, enters* R. *She carries her handbag*)

IRIS (*crossing to* C) Hallo, Ernie.

GIMLET (*intent on his game*) You all right?

IRIS. You heard about it, then?

GIMLET. Yes. (*He turns to Iris*) Iris . . .

IRIS. What?

GIMLET. How's your mother?

IRIS. She's all right. (*She sits above the left end of the table* RC) I feel a bit weak. D'you think you could get me a cup of tea?

GIMLET. Yes, of course. Cup of tea, Nellie.

(NELLIE *pours a cup of tea*)

NELLIE. With sugar?

GIMLET. Lots of sugar. (*He collects the tea from the counter and puts it on the table in front of Iris*)

(NELLIE *exits behind the counter*)

IRIS. Thanks, Ernie.

GIMLET. Feeling better now?

IRIS. I'm all right.

GIMLET. Good. Iris . . .

IRIS. What?

GIMLET. Will you come to the pictures with me tomorrow night?

(IRIS *looks slowly up at him*)

What's wrong?

IRIS. Is that all you have to say to me?

GIMLET. What do you mean?

IRIS. I come in straight from an accident and all you're

interested in is whether I can go to the pictures with you.

GIMLET. But I don't . . .

IRIS. How egotistic can you get?

GIMLET. I asked how you were.

IRIS. Yes, while you played the pin-table at the same time. You couldn't waste the penny, could you?

GIMLET. I had it in my hand when you came in. I just let go, that's all. For goodness' sake, I've been waiting for you over half an hour. I've got to go in a few minutes.

IRIS. I'm very sorry. I apologize for being late.

GIMLET. What have I *done*?

IRIS. Nothing. You haven't done anything. (*She weeps*)

GIMLET. Shock.

IRIS. That's right, put it down to shock. That makes it all right, doesn't it?

GIMLET. Look, Iris . . .

IRIS. Oh, leave me alone. Go back to your pin-table.

(GIMLET *looks at Iris for a few moments, then goes to the pin-table.*

BERT DOGG, *a bus driver, enters* R. *His head is bandaged*)

DOGG (*crossing to* LC) Well, well, here I am.

GIMLET. Dogg . . .

DOGG. Hallo, Gimlet, old friend. You still here?

GIMLET. I've got five minutes yet. You timed it badly.

DOGG (*moving above the pin-table*) You're not playing that right.

GIMLET. Do you mind!

DOGG. Never win if you play it fair, you know. Have to jigger it about—like this, see? (*He pushes the machine*)

GIMLET. You've tilted it! You've . . . ! (*He is speechless*)

DOGG. Don't know me own strength, do I? You heard about my little error of judgement, I suppose? Happens to the best of us, that's what I say. (*He moves to Iris*) Iris, my pet, you're not looking at all well. How do you feel?

IRIS. I'm all right, Bert.

DOGG. You shouldn't have bothered to come back. Delayed shock, that's what this is. (*He picks up her cup*) Here, drink this tea.

(DOGG *holds the cup while* IRIS *sips the tea*)

IRIS. I'm all right, really.

DOGG. No, you're not. (*He puts down the cup*) Tell you what: you just sit there quietly for a few minutes while they sort this out in the office, and then I'll take you home and put you straight to bed. All right?

IRIS. If you say so, Bert.

DOGG. Not another word, then. Want something to eat?

IRIS. I'll wait till I get home.

DOGG. Sit quiet, then, while I get things straightened out. Won't be long. (*To Gimlet*) Look after her for a minute, will you, old friend? Here, she might like to look at the paper. (*He takes a newspaper from Gimlet's overcoat pocket and gives it to Iris*) Here you are, take your mind off it. Get her another cup of tea if she wants it. And don't make too much noise with that thing, will you? She wants to be quiet.

(DOGG *crosses and exits* R. GIMLET *looks at his watch and moves to Iris*)

GIMLET. Do you want another cup of tea?

(IRIS *shakes her head*)

Biscuit or . . . ?

IRIS. No, thanks.

(GIMLET *hovers* L *of Iris*)

You don't have to stay.

GIMLET. I won't if you don't want me to.

IRIS. I didn't say I didn't want you to.

(*There is a pause.* GIMLET *takes out a cigarette and lights it*)

I haven't seen you around lately.

GIMLET. That's the way it goes, isn't it? You won't see me at all after this week.

IRIS. What?

GIMLET. I'm getting my cards.

IRIS. What's happened?

GIMLET. Nothing's happened. I'm just packing the job in.

IRIS. Why?

GIMLET. Why not? There's nothing in it for me here.

IRIS. What are you going to do?

GIMLET. Go back to baking, I suppose.

IRIS. I thought you didn't like baking.

GIMLET. What's that got to do with it?

IRIS. If you're not happy in the job . . .

GIMLET. Happy! I'm not meant to be happy. I'm not one of the blokes who's supposed to be happy.

IRIS. That's a silly way of looking at it.

GIMLET. No, all right . . .

IRIS. I mean, I don't think it's a very mature attitude.

GIMLET. No, well, I'm only a lad, you see. My ambition, of course, is to be a really mature man of the world like Bert Dogg.

IRIS. I wasn't thinking of Bert. (*She pauses*) Well, I hope you get on all right.

GIMLET. What?

IRIS. Making doughnuts.

GIMLET. Thanks very much. (*He pauses*) You don't like me, do you?

IRIS. What makes you say that?

GIMLET. It's just suddenly occurred to me.

IRIS. I didn't think you were interested in what people thought of you. *Too.*

GIMLET. No, that's right. Hell, hell!

IRIS. What's the matter with you, Ernie Gimlet?

GIMLET. D'you really want to know? I've just realized. I'm nobody who wants to be somebody, that's all. That's what's the matter with me.

IRIS. I don't understand you.

GIMLET. Don't bother; it's not worth it.

IRIS. I'm washing my hair tomorrow night, anyhow.

GIMLET. I thought you probably would be.

IRIS. I always wash my hair on a Friday.

GIMLET. How interesting!

IRIS. What are you angry about?

GIMLET. I'm not angry.

IRIS. Then don't shout.

GIMLET. I'm not angry. I'm just sick of—everything being so ordinary. I'm sick of being—being . . .

(*There is a pause*)

IRIS. You don't know what you're sick of, do you? You don't know *what* you want. (*She pauses*) Everything's wrong for you, isn't it?

GIMLET. I've got two minutes. Let's not . . .

IRIS. It's all wrong for you. The whole world. You ask whether I like you; how can I like you? When you do nothing but brag and bellyache. The trouble is I'm fond of you. But I don't like you. I suppose you think yourself a mixed-up kid. Well, you're a bit bloody old to be a mixed-up kid.

GIMLET. Please don't swear.

IRIS. Why shouldn't I?

GIMLET. Because it makes you ordinary. Like everyone else. Like me. (*He goes to the pin-table and searches in a distracted way amongst his change for a penny*)

IRIS. Is that it?

GIMLET. Leave me alone.

IRIS. D'you want a penny? We're all ordinary. What do you expect? Glamour?

(LILLIAN *enters* R)

LILLIAN (*crossing to* C) Mr Gimlet—I hate to break into your afternoon, but I thought you might like to know we have a bus full of passengers waiting your convenience, and we're due out in thirty seconds' time.

(GIMLET *gives Lillian a long look*)

Don't look at *me*; it's not my fault. Well, are you coming, or shall I give your apologies to the passengers? (*She pauses*) May I have an answer?

GIMLET. Miss Fitch, we've been getting on each other's nerves for some months. Even you must have cottoned on to the fact I'm just not *original* enough to walk out on a bus-load of passengers, much as I'd like to. I'm just an ordinary bus-driver like all the rest. So why don't you quit pestering me?

LILLIAN. We're in agreement at last. I had the idea you considered yourself something exceptional. I'm glad to know you've changed your mind. I shall be on the bus when you decide to come.

(LILLIAN *exits* R)

GIMLET. No, not glamour.

IRIS. What?

GIMLET. I said it wasn't glamour I wanted.

IRIS. If you like, I'll put off washing my hair and we'll . . .

GIMLET. Go ahead and wash your hair.

IRIS. But you wanted to . . .

GIMLET. Look, I'm just a bloody misery; I'm immature, see. I shall spend my life wanting things I can't have. You wash your hair; it'll be something accomplished. You won't accomplish anything with me.

IRIS. But I don't want to wash my hair, any more.

GIMLET. Then go to the pictures with Bert Dogg.

IRIS. You're being rather petty.

GIMLET. Exactly. You hang on to Bert Dogg. He's a steady bloke. He wants what he's got. He doesn't worry about what he's turning into. He's mature, see?

IRIS. I don't *want* to go to the pictures with Bert.

GIMLET. Then wash your hair. (*He collects his coat and cap*) I've got to go. (*He puts on his coat*)

IRIS. What's the *matter* with you? I'm not *tied* to you. I hardly even *know* you. We've only been out *twice* together. And we're acting as though we're . . .

GIMLET. Married.

IRIS. Hm?

GIMLET. Quarrelling as though we're married. (*He pauses*) You know old Nimrod? (*He points up* R) Bloke who always sits over there. Cheese sandwiches and a thermos flask. He was my age, once. A young man. Larked about; had ideals. Thought it was just a matter of time before he got what he wanted. He was just waiting for the day. He must have looked at people who were like he is now and said, "Not for me. I'm for something else than that. I'm going to make life what I want it to be." But *he's* sitting there now, and I'm looking at him like he used to look at those other blokes. And in twenty years' time *I'll* be sitting there, and there'll be some other young bloke full of life, looking at *me*. "Oh, no," he'll say, "life's not gonna get *me* like that." And Fran? She was young once. *She* used to go out with her boy-friend with her eyes full of stars and her heart full of . . . Look at her, now. What d'you think happened? You think it was an accident? No—she just *grew* up. That's all. Like all the rest of them, all this shower of misery. You think we'll be any different? You'll be Fran, I'll be Nimrod. Don't you believe me? You think there's a way out? It's all a fraud, you see. Everything we want, everything we're brought up to value, everything we think we can hold in our hands and keep—none of it lasts, *none* of it. Name me something that lasts! It's all a fraud, don't you get it?

(*There is a pause*)

Iris. But, Ernie . . .
Gimlet. See you in twenty years' time.

(Gimlet *exits* r)

Iris. It's not true. (*She takes out a mirror from her handbag, stares into it and runs one finger along her brow*)

(Nellie *enters behind the counter*)

Nellie. Do you want another cup of tea, dear? While it's still hot.

(Iris *does not reply*.
       Dogg *enters* r *and crosses to* c)

Dogg. Well, it's all fixed. We've got the rest of the day off. Come on, I'll take you home.
Iris. All right. (*She rises*) No. (*She pauses*) Bert.
Dogg. What is it?
Iris. I don't want to go home. I'm feeling all right now.
Dogg. You sure?
Iris. I'm quite sure. Take me to the pictures, Bert.
Dogg. You really think you'll be . . . ?

IRIS. I've told you, haven't I? Do you want to take me to the pictures or not?

DOGG. Come on, then, my pet.

(DOGG *and* IRIS *exit* R. NELLIE *comes from behind the counter and clears the remaining plates, etc.*)

NELLIE. One thing's certain in this life: no matter what happens—weddings, razor-fights, Lord Mayor's Shows, fires, floods or just the plain ordinary everyday grind of earning bread and butter—the last thing you'll see, if you wait around long enough, will be some poor bleeder clearing up the mess.

(FRAN *enters behind the counter*)

FRAN. I never finished telling you what happened.

NELLIE. What to?

FRAN. Me. Last night. When I saw Sid.

NELLIE. Well, what did happen?

FRAN. Nothing. I went up to him where he was sitting there with this friend of his, and I said, "Hallo, Sid," I said. And he never even looked up. He just went on talking to this friend, as though he hadn't heard. As though I wasn't there. (*She pauses briefly*) I'll give you a hand with them things.

FRAN *comes from behind the counter as—*

the CURTAIN *falls*

FURNITURE AND PROPERTY LIST

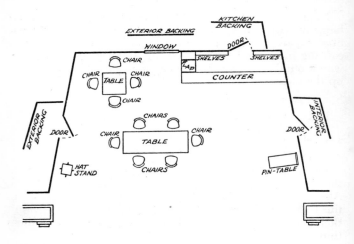

On stage: Counter. *On it:* glass case with cheese rolls, cakes, biscuits, etc., cups, saucers, teaspoons, sugar, milk, large pot of tea, cash till, cutlery, coffee urn

Table (RC) *On it:* menu, salt pot, pepper, mustard, vinegar, sugar, ashtray.

> *Above right end:* part finished plate of dinner, knife and fork
>
> *Above left end:* plate of steak and kidney pie and potatoes, knife and fork

Table (up R) *On it:* menu, salt pot, pepper, mustard, ashtray, sugar, vinegar

10 chairs

Hat-stand

Pin-table

On wall up C: clock

> *On shelves behind counter:* cigarettes, etc., including Weights and Woodbines, matches, Setlers, bottle of O.K. sauce
>
> Other suitable dressing

Off stage: Vacuum flask of tea (NIMROD)
Packet of sandwiches (NIMROD)
Bucket, mop, dust-pan and brush (FRAN)
Plate of fish and chips (NELLIE)
Plate of steak and kidney pie and potatoes (NELLIE)
Plate of jam tart and custard (FRAN)
Plate of fish and chips (FRAN)
Book (LILLIAN)
Plate of fish and chips (FRAN)

Personal: GRUNGE: watch, money
FRAN: copy of the *Daily Mirror*
INSPECTOR: notebook, watch
PUMFRET: 10/– note, 2 photographs
LILLIAN: handbag. *In it:* coins
NIMROD: coins, wallet with photograph
GIMLET: watch, coins, newspaper, cigarettes, matches
IRIS: handbag. *In it:* handkerchief, mirror